PASSIVE INCOME

Proven Steps and Strategies to Make Money While Sleeping

Mark Smith

This document is geared towards providing exact and reliable information in regards to the topic and issue covered. The publication is sold on the idea that the publisher is not required to render accounting services, officially permitted or otherwise. If advice is necessary, legal or professional, a practiced individual in the profession should be ordered.

- From a Declaration of Principles which was accepted and approved equally by a Committee of the American Bar Association and a Committee of Publishers and Associations.

The information provided herein is stated to be truthful and consistent, in that any liability, in terms of inattention or otherwise, by any usage or abuse of any policies, processes, or directions contained within is the solitary and utter responsibility of the recipient reader. Under no circumstances will any legal responsibility or blame be held against the publisher for any reparation, damages, or monetary loss due to the information herein, either directly or indirectly.

Respective authors own all copyrights not held by the publisher.

The information herein is offered for informational purposes solely and is universal as so. The presentation of the information is without a contract or any type of guarantee assurance.

The trademarks that are used are without any consent, and the publication of the trademark is without permission or backing by the trademark owner. All trademarks and brands within this book are for clarifying purposes only and are the owned by the owners themselves, not affiliated with this document.

Table of Contents

Introduction

I want to thank you and congratulate you for purchasing the book, *"Passive Income: Proven Steps And Strategies to Make Money While Sleeping"*.

This book contains proven steps and strategies on how to earn some extra cash without having to depend on your day job. In an age where economies are crumbling and jobs are being lost, you need to find new ways to use your time to make that extra buck. The idea of earning a secondary income is the way to go, and you can now leverage the advanced technology available to make money online. Passive income is not the wave of the future – it is already sweeping across the globe right now.

The first thing this book will teach is what passive income actually is. There are a lot of people who tend to get the wrong idea about what passive income really means. Here the record will be set straight. As you read this book, you will find yourself being asked some truly pertinent yet revealing questions about your passive income strategy. Be honest and think deeply about each one of these questions. They could end up determining whether you achieve success or failure.

This book will also define exclusively new and radical ways to develop a real passive income. You will learn how to make money on the side and still keep your day job if you wish. There are some strategies that will allow you to make money so fast that you may even be tempted to quit your day job and enjoy your life anew, doing the things that you really love.

One thing that has to be clearly understood is that this is not a get rich quick scheme. If you are expecting some kind of content on how to con people out of their hard-earned money, then this book is not for you. The strategies outlined here are simple business ideas and principles that you can leverage to create a passive income stream. If you can take the information in this book and implement the strategies, there is no reason why you should not succeed.

Thanks again for purchasing this book, I hope you enjoy it!

Chapter 1: What Is Passive Income?

In order to maximize your use of passive income to attain financial freedom, you have to first accurately understand the concept itself.

Passive vs. Active Income

Passive income is simply revenue that you earn without actively working for it. It is not like a regular job where you have to show up every day, put in time and effort, and may even get fired from. With passive income, money keeps on flowing in even if you do not go to work.

It is very different from active income, where you have a contract to work for a client or employer, and failure to do so results in loss of income. Some people tend to confuse the term passive income by including some types of "off-the-books" contract work. Just because the work you are doing offers you some kind of flexibility does not mean it is part of your passive income. As long as you have to do the work yourself, it is classified as active income.

The key thing to understand is that passive income allows you to get paid even though you are not actively engaged in doing any meaningful work. You may have to spend some time initially setting the business up and getting it off the ground, but there will come a time when you will be able to sit back and enjoy your passive income stream. You will actually have a choice of whether to continue working or not. An active income does not present you with this kind of freedom.

What Passive Income Is Not

There are some income streams that you may benefit from yet they cannot be truly categorized as passive income. A good example of this is receiving an inheritance or selling an asset. These are simply one-off lump sum payments that have no continuation over time.

Passive income is not necessarily risk-free. It cannot be defined as being totally secure income. Yes, there are some income streams that have less risk than others, but the truth is that every source of income carries some risk. Even with passive income, it is always wise to create multiple income streams in order to minimize the risk of failure.

Another thing that passive income is not is "maintenance-free." At some point in time, you will have to step in to carry out some kind of maintenance to keep the income stream flowing steadily. It is a myth to believe that once you establish your source of passive income and step back, you no longer have to keep an eye on things. There are taxes to be filed, checks to be deposited, and even mail to be responded to. It may be small things here and there but they still need to be done.

When looking at the level of maintenance required in sustaining passive income, you need to determine whether it is very passive or semi-passive. A good example is writing a book versus renting out your house. With a very passive income like book royalties, you dot really have to do much once the book is published. The book will be sold in stores or online by the publisher and you will not be required to deal with customers. All you will have to do is cash in the royalty checks. With a semi-passive income like house rentals, you will be required to maintain the house on a regular basis. You may also have to look for new tenants, make insurance payments and taxes, and even supervise the building caretaker.

Finally, passive income is not a get-rich-quick scheme. If you have the idea that you can create a passive income stream by cheating people off of their hard-earned cash, then this book is definitely not for you. This kind of mindset should not be used to define a passive income. There are people who try to look for ways to make money without necessarily providing anything of value in return. This is not entrepreneurship – it is plain thievery.

It is true that there are loopholes in the economy that you can leverage to make some money for yourself. However, this type of approach should never be described as a passive income. You should always try to create value for your customers so that they are always willing and ready to give you their money. There are some businesses that require you to provide more value than others, but at the end of the day, you need to offer something to get money in return.

Key Questions To Ask yourself
Where will passive income streams lead me?

A lot of people jump into developing multiple income streams without clearly defining what their end game will be. You need to ask yourself how your life will respond to the successes you will achieve. How will that extra $1000 change your life? At what point will you be able to live off of your passive income? How will you spend your spare time once you start earning money passively?

Is passive income a recipe for success or failure in my life?

Would you invest your extra time and money on productive things in your life or would you laze around, get fat, do drugs, and ultimately die early? These are pertinent questions you cannot afford to skip. You need to decide how you will grow your life and share the value you have created with others around you. Otherwise, you will simply be tempted to engage in things that will bring you down faster than you came up. Many people have burned out or become depressed because they did not plan in advance how they would structure their new life.

Why do I need passive income streams?

What motivations do you have for creating passive income? Is it simply because you are constantly broke or in debt? You need to realize that your motivation for wanting that extra money is what will determine what your life looks like after you get it. The truth is that in most cases, you can still be happy with the little money you have, so ensure that your motivation is linked to attaining fulfillment and contentment.

Avoiding the Hype

There are many books and web articles out there that claim to teach you how to make a lot of money quickly. They may even say that their system is guaranteed to give you a passive income stream for free. You need to be careful with such schemes. A lot of innocent people have been swindled and lost money by falling for such strategies.

This book is not about creating money from thin air. There is something that will always be required of you when creating a passive income stream. These include time, energy, money, and commitment. Passive income always involves work, so do not get the wrong idea because you are desperate to pay your rent by next week. Making passive income work for you will require that you get down and dirty in the initial stages and make sacrifices just like every truly successful businessperson. There are no shortcuts in this book. Do the work first, and then start thinking about enjoying the results. Now let us take a look at some of the ways in which you can create a passive income that will transform your life, and take you one step closer to financial freedom!

Chapter 2: Invest In Real Estate

When you decide to venture into real estate investing to generate passive income, you have to consider what kind of approach to use. There are different strategies that you can leverage in order to find an approach that suits not just your financial needs but also your startup capital investment.

Turnkey Real Estate

A really good way to start generating passive income in real estate is through turnkey rental properties. Turnkey properties can be a golden opportunity for anyone who wants to start investing in real estate. So what are turnkey properties and why are they so special?

Turnkey real estate properties are simply properties that have already been renovated, usually by a property management company, and are on sale. You purchase the property from the real estate management company and rent it out, earning yourself a tidy sum every month. What makes this type of real estate investment popular is that the same company that managed the property before can provide you with management services after the sale. They will collect your rent, pay for maintenance and repairs, handle all the documentation, and send you your money. You do not have to deal with the renters yourself, so this saves you time and effort.

However, there are certain things that you have to consider as an investor before choosing this sort of passing income vehicle:

Research the Property

You have to know your property well before deciding to buy it. This means that you need to conduct proper research to determine whether the house is worth buying. You need to ask yourself if the value of the home is really what the seller is describing. A lot of rookie investors jump at the chance to buy a turnkey property only to realize that the property wasn't worth it.

The best way to know your property is to visit it in person and check it out. If the property is in another part of the country, you may have to send someone you trust to take a look at it, or even travel there yourself. Buying real estate is a massive investment that you cannot take lightly, and you need to make sure that what you get is of the same value as the money you are putting down. Visit the area and get a feel of how the place will develop in the future. Will the property still retain or increase its value considering the current trends in the neighborhood, or will its value drop?

You should consider what your cash flow will look like once you buy the property and rent it out. Choosing a property in a poorly kept neighborhood just because expenses will be low and income high is a bad idea. A high return always carries a high risk. You will be better off going for property that is in a well-kept area with good social amenities, even though monthly profits may be lower. Your property is more likely to appreciate in value with time.

It is also a good idea to involve a professional property inspector so that they can examine the details that most property management companies will not willingly reveal to you. You may be impressed by the finishing and renovations on the home, but what about the roof, HVAC system, or the plumbing behind the walls? A professional home inspector will be able to note down things that you may not see.

Get to know the character of tenants in the neighborhood

As a potential landlord, you do not want to have tenants who give you a headache every day. You need to visit the neighborhood to know the kind of tenants that live in the area. Tenants who are stable and responsible will be more reliable when it comes to paying rent on time. Some areas have tenants who break or damage property and move out without giving any notice.

Research the Vacancy Rates

Always make sure that you know the vacancy rate of the property you are investing in. A home or apartment with a high vacancy rate will not bring in a lot of money. It may be of high value or have the potential to appreciate in the future, but you also need to think about your property expenses. You are better off buying property that is able to bring in tenants on a regular basis.

Research the Property Management Company

There needs to be a lot of trust between you and the property management company. If you are going to work with them, then you need to have faith that they are experienced professionals who can be trusted to handle your issues. There is nothing as bad as dealing with a management firm that doesn't carry out repairs when they need to, or isn't diligent enough to look for new tenants. It is critical that you do a background check to determine certain aspects of the way the firm operates, such as:

- The fees that they charge

- Whether they provide monthly statements to help you monitor the income and expenditure on the property

- The time it takes them, on average, to fill rental property vacancies

- The years of experience they have

This information can be obtained by sitting down and talking to the property manager, but it would help you more if you talked to other clients who have worked with the firm.

Understand the Type of Agreement

You need to know what kind of ownership agreement you are getting into with the management firm. It could be that they want their name to stay on the title, so instead of selling you the property, they opt to become your partner through an LLC. It is in your best interests to buy the property outright to prevent future problems, so the recommended solution, in this case, would be to create an independent expense account to be used for maintenance purposes when necessary.

Understand the Potential Risks

Investing in real estate may be lucrative, but it definitely isn't for everyone. You should always be prepared for any risks or problems that may arise, for example, unforeseen property tax hikes. You need to have some money on hand just in case something unforeseen happens. Most people who choose to invest in real estate tend to do so for the long-term. There are always ups and downs in the property market, and it is best to be patient when investing in this sector. If you cannot do so, then you need not bother putting your money in real estate.

Making Money Through Airbnb

Airbnb is a peer-to-peer service that allows you to rent out your house or apartment for a short period of time. It is a great way to make some extra cash especially when you have room in your house that isn't being used. You may also be planning to go out of town for a while yet the rent still has to be paid, so why not rent out your apartment for the duration?

The Airbnb app allows you to list your property – which can be anything from a single room to a houseboat – on the Airbnb website for free. You can then promote your property by creating a profile with titles, descriptions, and photos. This information then helps guests to find a suitable place to stay in case they are in the area. Airbnb helps you connect to other people in the area who are looking for temporary housing.

A guest may go through the database by filling in details of where they are traveling to and when they will be in the area. How attractive or interesting your property will be to guests may depend on the type of room/space on offer, your rental price, the size of the space available, any amenities you may be providing, or even the language that you speak.

So how do you go about setting up a business using Airbnb?

Listing your Space

You are the one who decides when to rent out your space and the price to charge as rent. The listing process is free, and you can choose whom to rent to by approving potential tenants in advance. You will have to keep in mind that there are other people who may be renting out their spaces, so keep your price competitive.

You need to look at the costs of hosting a guest, for example, cleaning, utility bills, Airbnb's host charges, and taxes. If you intend to use the Airbnb service, you will need to comply with their hosting standards and regulations. These include how to list your property accurately, how to communicate with your tenants, maintaining your reservation obligations, hygiene standards, and provision of basic amenities like toilet paper and soap.

Your listing on the Airbnb website will include a photo of the room or house, so make sure that it is neat and presentable. You can take the picture yourself and upload it, or Airbnb may send a professional to take photos free of charge, though this is only for active hosts. You can even cross-promote your space on social media or via your personal website.

The way you describe your space will determine the level of interest it generates on the platform. Describe it in a unique way and from the perspective of someone who is not a local. This means that you should emphasize the nearest transit means available, the nearest entertainment spots and restaurants, and what the culture is like in the area. You should also elaborate on any additional benefits a guest may benefit from, such as cable TV, Wi-Fi, a fully stocked fridge, etc.

Getting Authorization and Paying Taxes

If you are renting an apartment or house and want to take in a paying guest, then you will have to get permission from your own landlord. In case your property is part of a co-op or homeowners' association, then you need to make sure that there is nothing in their rules that disallows hosting a paying guest. Airbnb always recommends that you add a rider to any contract you sign with the above entities to specifically deal with hosting via Airbnb.

There are also local income taxes to think about. The local authority may consider anybody renting out his or her space using Airbnb to be running a hotel, so there could be a transient occupancy tax to pay. You will also have to pay federal taxes.

Personal Security

If you are renting out a room in your apartment or house, you should carefully consider your personal safety. In case you are going on a trip, then you will have the headache of locking away anything of high value, just in case your guest has itchy fingers. It is recommended that you find out more about your tenant by looking at reviews written about them by previous hosts. You may also do some basic Internet detective work, or run a criminal background check (if you realistically can).

Payment Guarantees

Payment is done via Airbnb, and your money is released to you within 24 hours of the arrival of your guest. If there is something that the guest isn't happy with, they are allowed to report it to Airbnb within 24 hours to get a refund. Trying to get paid outside the Airbnb system is a bad idea as the guest can easily dupe you. In the event that you are caught receiving payments outside the platform, Airbnb reserves the right to stop doing business with you.

Creating a passive income stream via Airbnb is a great way for you to meet different and interesting people while making some extra money. You can easily rent out one of your spare rooms in your house for a short period of time, thus helping you to pay the bills or have some residual income. Investing in real estate via Airbnb maximizes the use of your real estate property as the rent will still be paid even when you aren't around.

Chapter 3: Create a Website and Start Blogging

There are a lot of people who have tried to make money online by setting up a website – and failed miserably. Then there are others who have been so successful doing it that they quit their day jobs and became passive income earners. What was the difference? The first group just didn't do it the right way.

Is it possible to make serious money by starting a blog, and if so, how do you do it? The truth is that you can definitely make a lot of money through creating a website and blogging. The secret is to use the right strategies and find the best way to monetize your efforts.

A great blog is all about content. If you have great content, people will keep coming back to your site and you will be able to make more money. A lot of people spend too much time trying to fool the Google search bots to popularize their site, but this approach is doomed to fail in the long-term. These are the guys who go around saying blogging can't generate passive income.

But the successful ones know how to do it the right way. You can either have a website that sells products or dispenses information. Whichever option you choose, go for something that you are passionate about and keep tweaking your strategy until you get it right. As long as you focus on producing content that your readers find valuable, you will be able to draw in more people and make tons of money.

So what are some of the strategies that you can use when trying to make passive income through blogging?

Contextual Pay Per Click Advertising

With Pay Per Click (PPC) advertising, you can use either Google AdSense or Yahoo Publisher Network (YPN).

Google AdSense is more popular because they will only show ads that are relevant to the niche that your blog caters for. It is also the easiest option to put in place.

YPN is a major competitor to AdSense. YPN, however, does not display ads that are as relevant to your content as Google does, so this might not appeal to your site visitors. On the other hand, YPN pays you more per click than AdSense, so it becomes a question of balancing short-term goals with long-term passive income.

If you are unsure of which one to pick, just start with the simplest option, AdSense, and test it out. Place the ads in different places on your site and move them around regularly. Monitor how effective the placement is. You can also change the color of the text or link to see how visitors respond to these alterations. Do not make multiple changes at the same time because if traffic skyrockets, there will be no way of knowing which change caused the upsurge. After a couple of months, you can change to YPN and track the changes in traffic levels. Testing different techniques and strategies is a great way to figure out what works best for your site.

Affiliate Marketing

The most successful Internet marketers use this strategy. A lot of people have tried to use this strategy, but the problem is that they used wrong techniques, failed to put in enough effort, and gave up midway. Picking the right system to use can keep you rolling in dough for a really long time.

The first step is to know your niche thoroughly. If your blog is about fitness, make sure you become an expert at it. The content that you place on your blog needs to be of high quality and authoritative. Readers can smell BS by simply reading your content and examining the facts presented.

Once you do this, it's time to find great products to promote.

Not just any products, but the ones that are selling really well. The simplest affiliate program out there is ClickBank. You sign up and then search for any products that your blog can promote via keywords, and receive a code that allows you to promote that product. There is also Commission Junction, which actually gives you better insights to the number of clicks you have sent, though the products on offer are not as hot as those on ClickBank.

Monetize by Displaying Ads

There are some bloggers out there who seem to have a problem with this strategy because they think placing ads on your site cheapens the content. The question you need to ask yourself is this – Are you willing to provide people with free and high-quality content and not get paid for it? You are reading this book because you want out of the regular 9 to 5 rat race. If you can get paid for writing about stuff that you actually enjoy, why not do it?

You need to start by producing great content for your readers, the kind of content that people find helpful and useful to their lives. Most visitors expect successful sites to have some ads, and the fact that you do not have any ads may make them think that you are not popular or authoritative enough. You do not have to charge visitors subscription fees or sell them anything. Ads can make you a lot of money while making your site seem credible.

So what is the best time to place ads on your blog? Should you wait until traffic reaches a certain number of visitors per day, or just dive right in? You need to look at it this way: If you wait until you have a specific number of hits per day, then that day may never come. The best strategy is to do it immediately. Why? The reason is simple. The moment you monetize your website and place ads on it is the moment you will get serious about producing great content to drive traffic. If you have a day job then it's highly likely that you won't have the time or energy to blog consistently. This will affect your traffic numbers. Placing ads from the get-go motivates you to start taking things seriously because there is money involved now.

Where you place your ads on your blog is not very important. You just have to tweak things regularly to find the best fit. Just make sure that the kinds of ads you allow on your blog are relevant to your content. The ads have to be useful and valuable to your visitors. Lack of relevancy will annoy and drive visitors away, and you will not make any money.

The best way to draw in advertisers to buy space on your blog is to create a page on your site that clearly explains how they can do so. In case an advertiser comes across your site, they can easily know your rates, the spots on offer, and how to buy your ad space.

Paid Text Link Adverts

This is a system where you sign up, search for link ads to place on your site, and get paid every time someone buys a link from your site. There are a lot of websites that use this strategy to generate revenue. You literally get paid to place links on your website.

The procedure is simple: Go to www.text-link-ads.com, sign up with them, fill in a form, and receive a tiny code snippet that you will then place in your blog. The name of your blog is then added to their marketplace. Whenever someone goes to the marketplace to buy links and decides to purchase them from your site, you receive an email. You then have to log into the Text-link-Ads marketplace to approve the ad. You will then get paid 50% of the revenue earned and the other 50% goes to text-link-ads.com as a fee. The key here is to set a good price for links on your blog. Make sure that you value your blog properly by comparing it to others in the same niche.

Sponsored Reviews

As a blogger, you can actually get paid to write reviews about products or services related to your content niche. If you are able to develop strong credibility with your readers, they will be more likely to believe you when you review a product or service. When a product seller or service provider sees just how credible you are and the large following you have, they will pay you to write a positive review of whatever they are trying to sell. Your readers might then be interested in finding out more about the product or service, and this generates potential sales for the seller.

There are a number of sponsored review marketplaces that you can sign up to, such as ReviewMe. This sponsored review website (www.reviewme.com) allows you to sign up, fill out a form, and they then add you to their marketplace. In case someone wants you to review his or her product, you receive a notification and can then negotiate a fee in exchange for a sponsored review.

Amazon Affiliate Program

This is a very popular affiliate program for Internet marketers. It is really easy to set up and you can start making money right away. You can place Amazon affiliate links on your site every time you write about a product that is being sold on Amazon.com. Everybody is familiar with Amazon as a great place to buy products, so referring people to the website will get you paid. The only issue with this strategy is that Amazon is very stingy with their fees. You only get paid 5% of the revenue that is generated via your blog. No other website pays this low.

However, it is still worth signing up. Sooner or later you will find yourself mentioning or reviewing a product that can be bought at Amazon. Placing a quick link to the product page on Amazon will help your readers gather more information while earning you a small sum at the same time.

Chapter 4: Create Online Video Tutorials

If you have a particular process or concept that you are really good at, and own a blog with relevant content, you may want to consider teaching it to people through a video tutorial. Leveraging the power of online videos is one of the best ways to get the word out about your skills in a particular niche. Videos tend to attract huge followings these days, and creating an online video tutorial can be a great way to earn passive income.

Creating a good quality video tutorial is not that complicated. If you know your niche well, adopt the right strategy, and use the right tools, you will quickly be viewed as an expert and develop a large online following. Before you begin making a video tutorial to earn some money, there are a number of factors that you have to consider.

Factors to Consider

Target Audience

This is one of the most important factors to consider before creating any kind of content. If you take the time to ask yourself who your target audience is, you will have a great chance to produce content that is valuable and useful. You need to look at the kind of content that you want to share and ask yourself what type of audience would appreciate it the most. Get to understand your target audience, what they like, how they think, and what kind of format will suit them best.

Your Target's Goals

Once you understand who your target audience is, you should know the goals that they intend to accomplish. Are their goals in line with the content you want to provide? Will your tutorial help them move closer to their goals? If their goals become part of your goals, you will undoubtedly be in a better position to help them.

Resources and Tools Your Audience Need

People will be attracted to your online content because you offer them resources and tools they need. That is part of creating value for your customers, as these resources and tools can help them achieve whatever goals they have. For example, if your audience is interested in learning how to assemble a home solar power kit, they are going to need a list of equipment to purchase, where to buy them, the prices, and safe assembly instructions. Your objective should then be how to help them acquire such information as easily as possible. Your video tutorials should be tailored towards bridging the gap between them and the resources they need.

Potential Affiliate Partners

The main aim of creating a video is to make money. This means that you will have to promote a product or service to your audience in exchange for cash. That is where affiliate programs come in. You should sign up for an affiliate program with companies that offer such partnerships so that you promote their products on the video and they pay you in return. It is important to note that having a decent-sized online following will help you negotiate how much you earn, and even open up doors to companies that do not have affiliate programs in place.

How to Plan your Process

You cannot dive right into making a video tutorial without having some sort of plan. This is where you sit down with pen and paper and think about what you are trying to accomplish using the video. How do you do this?

Know your Subject Matter

You must have complete in-depth knowledge of your subject matter. If you aren't yet well versed in that area, do your due diligence and get up to speed with what you need to know. A half-baked teacher will never be able to convince students that they know what they are talking about. Visit other blogs and forums relevant to your niche and look at the questions people frequently ask. Ask yourself what kind of problems or challenges your target audience tends to face and read up on that.

Prepare a Script

It is always a good idea to sound natural on video, but having a bullet-point script as a guide is critical in keeping you on point and reminding you of the next topic to be covered. You do not want to start figuring things out in the middle of a tutorial video. Proper planning will always help you create something unique and valuable.

Choose the Type of Video

You can decide to record your computer screen and guide the audience on how to perform specific actions. For example, you can show them how to sign up for an affiliate marketing program on a website. If you are using a screen recording, then you must make sure that the desktop background is clean. The computer display should not show any of your personal information or irrelevant programs running in the background. For screen casting options, you should consider high-quality programs like VirtualDub, Camtasia, ScreenFlow, or Camstudio.

Your video tutorial may incorporate you standing in front of the camera. If this is your mode of choice, you will need a DSLR, camcorder, or simply use your Smartphone.

You can also make video recordings using a slide show presentation. This is a great way to teach your audience as long as you can create your slides well. You can use software like Google Slides, MS PowerPoint or Keynote.

Your final option in choosing your video format is to combine two or more of the above formats.

Prepare your Audio

You can choose to record your audio via your computer's microphone, though the quality may not be that good. A good quality USB microphone may come in handy, and you don't have to go for an expensive one at all. An Audiotechnica microphone will only set you back $30.

A great acoustic environment means no loud gadgets humming in the background. Make sure that the surfaces do not reverberate sound and create an echo. If you want to have some interesting background music, you can go to any creative commons sites (for example ccmixter.org) that offer free licensed music. Make sure that your background music does not drown out or interfere with your voiceover.

Create your Affiliate Program Link

You can use the Pretty Link Plug-in on Wordpress to create a link that will enable you to make money from your video. This is the link that your audience will click on to go ahead and purchase any of the products or services you may have promoted in the video.

How to Create the Video

Once the planning process is complete, you can go ahead and record, edit, and export your video.

Recording your video tutorial should be easy now that you are familiar with the software and the format to be used. Just press the "Record" button and talk to your audience. Try to be friendly and create a personal connection with your audience. Just don't go overboard with theatrics as you may frustrate some of your serious viewers.

When it comes to editing your video, you need to use good software, some of which are paid while others are free. You can use ScreenFlow, iMovie, Adobe Premiere, or Final Cut Express. With great editing techniques, you can offer more value to your audience. You can highlight the important features, add text to ensure the smooth and clear flow of information, or even remove mistakes in the video recording. A well-edited video will always transition well and stick to the point. Any unnecessary pauses, delays in loading, or slip-ups in speech should be cut out. In case you cannot edit the video yourself, you should consider outsourcing the work to a professional.

Exporting your video simply means converting it from the editing format into a format that can be easily uploaded onto your video streaming platform (YouTube, Udemy, etc.).

How to Publish the Video

When it comes to choosing which video streaming service to use for your online content, you can never go wrong with YouTube. Remember, you want to make money from your video, so you need to use a platform that is the second largest search engine on the web. The traffic that goes through YouTube every day is insanely huge, and you have the opportunity to tap into it for free. You can also post the video tutorial on Udemy or your own business blog.

How to Optimize the Video

The title of your video is the most critical part of the video, for obvious reasons. You want to be found easily on the Internet, so make sure that you use SEO and relevant keyword in your title and description. Make sure that people and the search engines will know exactly what your video contains. Don't forget to place a link to your website within the description area to enable people to visit your site. You should also write a blog post based on the same topic and embed the video into it.

How to Promote your Video Tutorial

There are various ways to promote your video tutorial. You can:

- Send it to your email list
- Promote it on the sidebar or navigation bar of your blog
- Share it on social media
- Share it with other bloggers who have a similar audience
- Share it with companies whose products you can promote

Videos are a great way to reach millions of people worldwide. Viral videos are making a huge impact on people, so you can never go wrong with making a video tutorial.

Chapter 5: Sell Digital Informational Products

The Internet has totally revolutionized the way people buy and sell products. This has had the effect of opening up the world to everyone who has something valuable to offer, whether it's a product or a service.

When it comes to earning a passive income online, one of the best things to do is to sell a digital product. With just a little effort put in, you can be able to create an informational product and sell it at an affordable price. Think of all the products on sites like Amazon, Etsy, or EBay. The digital products on these online selling platforms are very cheap and the demand keeps soaring year after year. If you can create an awesome informational product and sell it online, you can earn money for years.

What is an Informational Product?

An informational product is simply a product that is created to provide more information or knowledge about a specific topic or theme. Think of things like eBooks or videos that teach you how to do something. An informational product gives you the opportunity to create value for your customers in a quick and easy way.

There are two fundamental reasons why creating and selling an informational product is a great idea:

- It enables you to make passive income without having to invest too much time. Think of it this way. Once you finish creating that "How-To" eBook or video, you simply sell it on a digital platform like Amazon.com or your own website, and move on to other things. Better yet, if you are offering some kind of service through a website, you can create an informational product to accompany your services, and thus add value to your existing business. Informational products tend to sell themselves. That's the beauty of online platforms. You can even take a break from running your business and still be comfortable knowing that your digital informational product is out there selling itself and making money.

- A digital informational product allows you to reach potential clients who are on a low budget or aren't sure whether to work with you or not. By referring them to your informational product, you can allow them to use your know-how at an affordable price, and thus build trust over time. Once they know that you have the expertise in a certain area and trust you, they are more likely to come back to purchase more products or services from you. Furthermore, they are also likely to refer you to other clients. An informational product can be shared with others and easily generate positive reviews for you. You have suddenly locked in current and future clients.

Factors to Consider before Creating an Informational Product

When deciding on what kind of informational product to create, you will have to look at your personal interests, business interests, the amount of time you have, and the needs of your target customers. Creating a passive income may be a great way to earn money easily over the long-term, but it still involves a lot of work in the initial stages.

You will have to take into account things like the length of time the product will take to create, the initial financial investment required, and the amount of money you would like to make in profits per hour.

There's an old saying that says, "You write what you know."

When deciding what to write about or create a video about, the best bet you can make is to create a product that you are knowledgeable about. At this point, there are two things to think about:

- Commonly asked questions

In whatever business or line of work you are engaged in, there are certain questions that clients constantly ask. You can talk to customers about their concerns, or visit the FAQ page of a relevant website in the niche you want to tackle. Instead of answering questions via long emails, you can cash in by writing an eBook or creating an online video explaining everything that clients need to know.

- Basic services that you can provide

There are probably certain basic services that you perform day in day out. If you have a website and find yourself outgrowing certain services, you can create videos of how to perform those services for your clients. If a client with a small budget comes and wants to hire you to do something for them, you can simply ask them to purchase and download the video. It will be cheaper for the customer and allows you time to engage in other activities.

Creating Your Informational Content

Writing an eBook

The great thing about selling an eBook is that you do not have to be a writer to do it. If you are an SEO expert, you can get a freelance ghostwriter to write the book for you. The same applies to you if you are a designer or software developer. It doesn't matter what your expertise is. If you can put your knowledge in written format that can be digitized and monetized, you will always find someone willing to buy it. EBooks are pretty hot right now, and you can never go wrong with them.

Making Audio and Video Content

You can make podcasts or videos where you give people information that is not easily found. You do not have to be an expert, because no matter how little you know, there is always someone else who knows less than you. If the price is right, customers will choose to buy from you.

Creating an Online Community or Forum

If you have a lot of information that you are willing to share with an exclusive group of people, you can create a members only pay-for-admittance forum. The website should have a constant flow of relevant and high-quality information that people would be willing to pay good money for. If you are a guru in start-ups, SEO, stock trading, etc., you can charge your members to gain access to top-notch information that cannot be found elsewhere. Your members will be able to download exclusive content, tips, job leads, or business advice. If successful, you can even hire assistants and moderators to help you out.

Teaching an Online Class

You can create a course outline composed of modules and worksheets in the form of slides. These can be downloaded for a fee and people can study them on their own. The challenge is in the beginning, as it may take a while to develop a good class outline that can be taught every week. However, once you have set everything up, things get easier. As long as you can make sure that the content on offer is updated and relevant, you can choose to recycle the preceding year's class notes.

How to Sell Your Products

Once you have created your informational product, you need to market it in order to generate enough interest. You will also have to decide how customers will be paying for the products before they download them.

When marketing your informational products, you need to focus on showing the customers the benefits of your content rather than just stating the features of the product. Tell people what they will get from your product and how it is unique. Make sure that your sales copy is easy to read through quickly and use images, bullets, and keywords. Keep your marketing emails short for those people who know you already.

There are certain tools that you can also use to help you sell your informational products:

- SendOwl – This is a monthly subscription platform that charges $9 per month. It is easy to learn and integrates many different payment processors, such as Authorize.net, stripe, and PayPal.

- E-junkie – This is a monthly subscription tool that costs $5 per month. It was one of the pioneer financial platforms for selling digital products. It is cheap if you are just starting an online business, and you can access your money via PayPal.

- Gumroad – This is a service that allows you to channel your customers to a specific page. You also have the option of embedding a link into the product you are selling on your landing page. It is a flexible tool that allows you to tweak the buttons to suit your website, so if you have web development skills, you will enjoy this option. Gumroad enables you to be paid via any of the major credit cards. You can access your money either through PayPal (once in a fortnight) or direct deposit. Since there are no monthly subscription fees, Gumroad is a good option for those sellers who are not yet sure just how many copies of a product will be sold per month. The service only charges you a 5% fee and an additional $0.25 for every transaction made. If you do not feel like committing to paying regular subscription fees, then this is the tool for you.

How to Adapt To Your Market

With time, you will discover that as your customer numbers grow, their needs also change. You should always have your finger on the pulse of your customer's needs so that you know when and how to adapt your informational products. Make adjustments to your products, whether it is by upgrading your course content, updating old information, or adapting to new trends.

If you are writing eBooks about SEO, you need to keep track of how Google adjusts its algorithms. If you are making videos, you could shoot new ones and include upcoming gurus instead of old ones. The key thing is to keep your content fresh. Earning passive income does not mean you have to play a passive role as others pass you by. Keep learning and stay in touch with what your customers want.

Chapter 6: Freelancing

More and more people are looking for new ways to earn more money every day. Having a regular job is not enough to meet today's needs, so freelancing has become one way to make some extra income.

There are a lot of things you can engage in as a freelancer. The beauty of being a freelancer is that you are able to offer your services in whatever area you are passionate about. If you hold a 9 to 5 job, you can use your time after work or weekends to diversify your income streams. With freelancing, you get to choose how to use your time and what to spend it on.

As a freelancer, you will have to determine what your strengths and weaknesses are so that you learn how to hone your craft and make the best use of your skills.

How to Freelance For Passive Income

There are a number of ways in which a freelancer can start earning a passive income. This will obviously depend on the kind of freelancer you are.

Selling Stock

Stock here refers to things like images, themes, scripts, and the like. If you happen to love photography, you can take pictures during your spare time and sell them to stock photography sites. Every time someone goes to the site and buys one of your photos, you get paid. You do not have to be a professional photographer to do this kind of work. With the advancements in Smartphone cameras, almost everyone is an amateur photographer. However, if you want to develop that cutting edge, it would be best if you learned some basic photography skills. Shutterstock is a good example of a website that can earn a good passive income for a photographer.

If you are a programmer, you can start writing scripts and sell them to any of the numerous script websites on the Internet. If you have a passion for web design, you can spend your free time creating templates, graphics, or Wordpress themes. This particular niche is getting more popular every year. It may sound a bit difficult for most people but if you are a designer, you can actually earn a substantial amount if you work on your own products and sell them. You can sell your stock graphics on your own website or to a marketplace. Examples of marketplaces that you can sell your stock themes, templates, and graphics include ThemeForest, GraphicRiver, and Creative Market.

These online marketplaces offer good prices for stocks, and you can make a minimum of $20 for just one template. In some cases, a template can be bought for $300, so the better your template is, the higher the earning potential.

Subscriptions and Memberships

Depending on the type of freelancer you are, you may have a lot of knowledge to share with the world. By signing up to a subscription service or membership area, you can offer your knowledge to customers in exchange for money.

A good example is the Envato network, which comprises a collection of websites and digital marketplaces that allow people with creative assets to offer or sell their ideas to others.

All you have to do is create a tutorial of whatever information or skills you want to share, sign up to the Envato network, and sell your content via their tutorial platform, Tuts+. Customers then subscribe to the network for about $9 per month and are allowed to download whatever content they are interested in. This is a very small price to pay for customers who are looking for high quality content, so if your work is top notch, you earn $9 per month for every subscriber.

Selling Advertising Space

You may have a steady job while also maintaining an active online presence via your personal website. If this is the case, then you should consider selling some of the space on your website to advertisers. This can be a great source of passive income if your website has a huge amount of traffic. Advertisers are always looking to reach greater audiences, and the number of visitors attracted to your blog or website will determine whether they will choose to work with you and how much you can make. As your website becomes more and more popular, you will be able to charge advertisers more money in exchange for posting their ads on your site.

Publish a Book

You do not have to be a writer to put your thoughts and knowledge into words. There are many ghostwriters on platforms like Upwork or Guru who can create a great book for you. Whatever area you are an expert in, writing a book can be a great way to make some passive income. You can self-publish on Amazon or use one of the many eBook services out there, such as e-Junkie.

Design Competitions

If you are into any kind of design, say web design, logo design, or designing flyers, you can enter a design contest. Design contests are not new, and they are a great way for amateurs to create a name for themselves. A design contest website such as 99Designs offers fantastic rates for logos, postcards, or website designs. There is always a design contest going on, so the opportunity to make some money is always available. However, you will have to work hard to make an impression on the contest creator and beat thousands of other competitors.

Chapter 7: Online Surveys

When it comes to making money online, it doesn't get simpler than online surveys. You do not have to make a financial investment or spend too much time setting up a business like the other methods mentioned in the preceding chapters.

Online surveys allow you to get paid every time you complete a survey, and this is something that can be done in tandem with your day job. Unlike a focus group, you do not need to have some kind of specialization to be eligible for paid online surveys. You can also take as many surveys as you like.

How to Use Survey Sites

- You register on any of the numerous online survey sites available. You will need to read the instructions carefully and understand how much you will be paid per survey. Some of the best survey sites in terms of money earned include GlobaltestMarket, SurveyHead, Ipsos, CashCrate, and ValuedOpinions.

- Once you have registered, you will start receiving emails from the survey website. The email will inform you of a survey that you qualify for. You do not automatically qualify for all surveys, and you will only be sent surveys according to the details you filled in during registration.

- Once you complete the survey, you are sent your payment via PayPal, check, coupons and special offers that can be used to buy stuff online.

The Do's and Don'ts of Paid Online Surveys

There are some basic rules that you can adopt to help you make this kind of passive income strategy a success. Some of them may be obvious and you may be knowledgeable about, while others are purely for your safety and security.

The Do's

- Do make sure that you always go to the survey website's privacy policy page and carefully read the fine print. A lot of people skip this step because they want to sign up and start making money really quickly. The danger is that you will never know how your personal information is going to be used, and ho your privacy may be potentially compromised.

- Do find out how much is paid per survey and the minimum payment amount that each site has. This will help you know how much you have to earn before you are allowed to cash out, and how quickly you can do so. There are some sites out there that set very high minimum payment amounts and pay you very little money per survey. When you are close to reaching the minimum amount for cashing out, they suddenly stop sending you surveys. You need to be careful that you don't end up wasting your time and energy on such sites.

- Do create a new email account completely dedicated to receiving emails regarding your paid surveys. You do not want to be swamped in different kinds of emails and fail to see the survey email in time. Some of these surveys are for a specific time frame and you may miss out.

- Do make sure that you check your mail on a regular basis so that your surveys don't pass you by. You can set up desktop alerts for that particular email account.

- Do take the time to update your profile regularly in order to keep receiving the most appropriate or relevant surveys for you. You want to be surveyed on things that you are interested in, and in case your interests change, you will need to update your preferences in your profile.

- Finally, do sign up to more than one survey site. This way, you maximize your chances of making as much money as possible. There will be times when some sites will not be sending regular surveys your way, and having other alternative options will help you go through that dry patch.

The Don'ts

- Do not pay any kind of membership fee to any survey site. Legitimate survey sites offer free sign-ups and do not ask for money upfront. If you come across any survey site that asks you to pay first, move along. They are definitely not legit.

- Do not give out personal information that is sensitive and can potentially be used against you. This includes credit card numbers, phone numbers, social security number, and the like. You do not want to fall victim to some kind of financial scam, or worse.

- Do not let your guard down when it comes to protecting yourself against viruses and spam. Some survey sites can easily expose your computer to viruses or Trojans, so make sure that you have the latest and updated antivirus tools. If you are going to be working online a lot, invest in protecting your computer.

- Finally, do not think that you can get rich and retire by simply filling in surveys. Paid online surveys are a great and easy way to make extra cash on the side, especially if you have the time. However, it is not a way to earn a stable living. Use it, but do not let it b your only source of passive income.

If you want to earn money via paid online surveys, you must have patience and dedication. This is not a get-rich-quick scheme that will make you a ton of money overnight. Be wary of the survey sites you visit and always look for the ones that are trusted and have the best reviews.

Conclusion

Thank you again for purchasing this book!

I hope this book was able to help you to discover just how to start making a passive income by doing what you love. This book has definitely opened up your eyes to the opportunities available.

The next step is to find the best way to monetize whatever passion you have. It may take some time, but you will soon be able to make money in your sleep!

www.ingramcontent.com/pod-product-compliance
Lightning Source LLC
Chambersburg PA
CBHW061051220326
41597CB00018BA/2849